Prayers Against Marine Spirits

Powerful Prayers and Declarations to Totally Destroy the Activities of Water Spirits

Dr. Olusola Coker

All Rights Reserved

This Book is Dedicated to God Almighty

Table of Contents

Introduction

The time has come to put a final stop on the activities of Marine Spirits. In recent times Marine Spirits has caused a lot of damages to the human race including Churches by influencing their behavioral pattern. Marine Spirits conduct their operation inside waters and made the oceans, rivers, seas, streams, and lakes their stronghold.

However, it is extremely difficult to detect Marine Spirits than any other Spirits including witchcraft spirit. Unlike Witchcraft spirits who are aggressive and impatient in their operation, Marine Spirit is different, they are patient, well mannered and cultured in their operation.

Are you finding solutions to any or all of the problems below but you find it difficult? Then this book is for you

Uncontrollable sex Uncontrollable masturbation Watching of pornographic videos Chronic Anger in You

1. Dead in everything in a man's life, eg, dead brain, dead organs, dead spiritual life.
2. The weakening of pastors power to perform a miracle or cast out demons
3. Inability to get married on time
4. Frequent divorce

5. Bankruptcy
6. Spirit wife
7. Spirit husband
8. Sex in the dre7am

Please find below the characteristics of Marine Spirits

Marine Spirits are wicked as witchcraft spirits

Marine spirits can wait for years to destroy their victims

Marine Spirits come in the form of beautiful ladies and they work with a purpose in mind Marine Spirits are always materialistic

Marine Spirits can make victim wealthy temporarily but later deal with them ruthlessly.

Marine spirits have their agents everywhere especially in Churches, who hide under the cover of church and lead people into immorality, fornication, lesbianism, homosexuals and so on. In some cases, Marine Spirit agents could be pastors, general overseer, and church leader and so on. Such pastors engage in various forms of an immoral act with Church members. You have to be careful about which church you attend.

Marine Spirit executes their plans by possessing either a man or a woman.

The marine kingdom is headed by the queen of the coast.

Marine Spirits possess female than male

There are two types of Marine Spirits. They are conscious and unconscious. The formal know they are possessed, while the latter doesn't.

Marine spirits use sex to oppress men and scatter homes through the power of sex.

Marine Spirits are extremely fashion-crazy, they dress to attract on purpose, they walk to attract on purpose.
Most ladies that date married men without remorse are Marine Spirits.
They enjoy breaking the hearts of their victims so as to render them emotionally unstable.
They make their victims take wrong decisions that will render their life useless.
Marine Spirits agents are very unstable in relationships and they cannot keep a relationship for too long.
Marine Spirits agents are good pretenders.
The worse thing that can happen to a man is to fall in love with a lady possessed with Marine Spirit.
If a man decides to end the relationship, the lady possessed with Marine spirit begins to behave well and the moment the man changes his mind, she starts tormenting the emotion of the man, constantly frustrating the man.
Lesbianism, homosexuality, and pornography are marine initiations
Marine Spirit agents are party goers

How do you know you are under the influence of a Marinespirit?

Number one way you can know if you are afflicted with marine spirit is through uncontrollable sex

When you sleep with a man or a woman you are not married to, you may be afflicted with Marine Spirit. If you dream that you are having sex with a known and or unknown man woman, then the marine spirit is at work in your life. In addition, when you sleep with an influential man or woman particularly celebrities, the marine spirit is operating in your life.

Prayer points

O Lord, I repent from my sins and that of my entire family including the sins of my forefathers, in the name of Jesus.

O Lord, my Father, have mercy on me and forgive me all my sins in the name of Jesus Christ.

O Lord, let my soul, my spirit and body be filled with the blood of Jesus Christ.

I eliminate every serpentine bite that I have received in my body through the dream in the name of Jesus Christ.

Agents of Marine spirit, what are you doing in my life, come out and die in the name of Jesus Christ.

You marine spirit hear the word of the Lord, lose your hold over my by the power in the blood of Jesus Christ.

O Lord, crush out every Marine spirit agent working against my marital favor, in the name of Jesus.

I totally bind every image representing me in the marine kingdom in the name of Jesus Christ.

I command the stubborn marine spirit spouse to be separated from me by the power in the blood of Jesus

You, Marine Spirit agent attacking my progress, I crush your head with the power of the Holy Ghost.

By the power in the blood of Jesus Christ, I separate myself from every ancestral covenant with water spirits in Jesus Name.

I burn to ashes every evil material transferred into my body through contact with marine witchcraft agents in the name of Jesus Christ.

Every arrow shot into my life by witchcraft powers from the waters, I soak you in the blood of Jesus and return you back to the sender, in Jesus name.

I roast to death by the fire of the Holy Ghost every marine spirit agent sent to disgrace me, in Jesus name.

Marine Spirit hiding in my house, be utterly flushed out by the Lightning of God today, in the name of Jesus Christ.

Today, I command every problem that has come into my life through contact with any marine spirit agent, to receive divine solution by the power in the blood of Jesus Christ.

I burn to ashes every strange eye of the marine spirits over my possession, in Jesus name.

Every marine spirit poison in my spirit, soul, and body, be purged out, in Jesus name.

Every linkage with the marine spirit with my life, break to pieces, in the name of Jesus.

Every covenant formed on my behalf with marine spirit by my ancestors/parents, break by the power in the blood of Jesus Christ.

Every python sent to destroy me, return to your sender, in the name of Jesus.

As a child of the Lion of Judah, I chase out every marine spirit from my life in the name of Jesus.

I burn to ashes every strange underground house in the water having my picture in Jesus name.

I burn to ashes the Pots of darkness in the water controlling my spouse in Jesus name.

I paralyze the Marine parasites, Marine virus, Marine bacteria hiding in my body in Jesus name.

I destroy by fire every spirit of seduction influencing my life negatively and delaying my marital glory, in Jesus Name.

I wash off every attraction of the serpent spirit to my life, by the power in the blood of Jesus Christ.

I burn to ashes all demons coiling around my head spiritually, in Jesus name.

I clean every pollution done to my financial blessing by the marine agents, by the power in the blood of Jesus Christ.

Every marine snail placed upon my legs; catch fire, in Jesus name

I burn to ashes every demonic possessed power attaching themselves to my glory, in Jesus Name.

Every crown of the queen of the coast upon my head is set ablaze in Jesus name.

I renounce the children of python out of my life, in Jesusname.

Every spiritual marriage, dowry, ring, gown given to me by the marine spirit, be dissolved by the blood of Jesus.

I withdraw all my information from the possession of the marine spirit kingdom, in Jesus name.

Any prolong delay in my life as a result of sexual contact with marine spirit agent be flushed out by the blood of Jesus, in Jesus name.

O Lord, every bewitchment from the water controlling my marriage shall die by fire, in the name of Jesus.

Any incision in my body, used as an entry point by marine spirit agents be flushed out by the power in the blood of Jesus Christ.

I withdraw my organ in the water used for sacrifice in Jesus name.

The strategy of water demons to separate me from my partner scatter by fire, in the name of Jesus.

I break and lose my self from marine covenant in Jesus name.

I burn to ashes the Certificates of spirit wife/husband in my domain in Jesus Name.

O Lord, end my marriage from strange waters in the name of Jesus Christ.

Any marine stronghold holding me down as a child of God, lose your grip over me, in Jesus name.

Every marine power operating at the edge of my destiny, I bury you alive today, in Jesus name.

Any evil priest connecting me with water gods from the marine kingdom, catch fire, in Jesus name

I bind and cast out of my life, every foul spirit troubling my deliverance, in Jesus name.

Marine spirit agents from the water monitoring me in my dream shall die by fire, in Jesus name.

I reverse every marine judgment and decisions ever taken against me, by the power in the blood of Jesus.

O Lord, I free myself free from every marine bondage, in Jesus name.

I command the Python spirit in my foundation attacking all women in my family, to die in Jesus Name.

Any household power that will not allow me to prosper dry up by the fire, in Jesus name.

Any ring cowries deposited in my body by marine spirit come out of me and catch fire, in Jesus name.

Spiritual children sucking my breast release and die by fire, in Jesus name.

Any of my hair attachment, lipsticks, indecent dressing that have initiated me into the marine coven burn in the name of Jesus.

A strongman from the marine kingdom assigned to monitor me you are a liar die by fire, in Jesus name.

Family marine altar catches fire and dies in the name of Jesus.

I challenge the forces of witchcraft serpent against my marriage to lose your hold and die, in Jesus name.

Materials from the marine kingdom, cowries, beads, jewelry inside my stomach, receive fire come and be roasted, in Jesus name.

Any stubborn chain from my father's house and mother's house binding me down to one spot catch fire, in Jesus name.

Spirit husband ruling over my marital breakthrough your end has come today, die by thunder.

Any name given to me by spirit husband or wife be changed by the blood of Jesus, in Jesus name. I command the Strong Goliath from the marine kingdom that has taken my dowry to return it and die, in Jesus name.

I cancel all decision and judgment of marine witchcraft over my life and family, in Jesus name.

Agenda of the marine spirit to paralyze my destiny-dreams, die by fire, in Jesus name.

Evil idols in my father's house bringing hardship and introducing financial wasters, catch fire.

I release myself from every evil inheritance, in the name of Jesus.

O Lord, flush out by the blood of Jesus Christ, every evil pronouncement that has been transferred into my foundation through evil covenant.

I reject any link between me and any river, in Jesus Name

I destroy every evil priest manipulating my life with marine witchcraft, by the power in the blood of Jesus Christ.

O Lord, I claim the anointing of God to destroy every marine spirit and their kingdom that come upon my life in Jesus name.

Thou jellyfish anointing inviting me to the river; die, in Jesus name.

Witchcraft oppression from my mother's house and my father's house and my place of birth, expire, in the name of Jesus.

Every Water goddess hindering my marital star shall die in Jesus Name.

O Lord, let Thunder of God strike down evil altars in the sea bearing my name, in Jesus name.

I throw down any fish of darkness revealing my greatness to goddesses, in Jesus name.

Familiar spirits cast upon me by spirit children; backfire, in Jesus name.

Crown of the queen of the coast placed upon my dream on my head catch fire, in Jesus name Power of marine witchcraft tormenting my reproductive organ; die, in Jesus name.

Calendar of spirit spouse updating my life for sex to a spirit husband/wife; catch fire.

Marine wedding gowns tormenting my physical wedding gown; catch fire, in Jesus name.

I dissociate myself from the use of marine materials by fire, in Jesus name

Number two way to discover you are under the control of a marine spirit is through uncontrollable Masturbation

Masturbation is an evil act and it is dangerous to the human race especially men. Most men these days have been rendered to the background through Masturbation. When you find it difficult to quit masturbating, the marine spirit is controlling your life. You need to pray for all the prayer points in this book to be set free. Masturbation due to the act of man or woman release their seed when the man's seamen are withdrawn and falls to the ground, it attracts Demon that create demon Larvae. According to God's word, Masturbation and Withdrawal are both one:

Facts you need to know about masturbation

Masturbation is the greatest sin ever

Masturbation is a very serious attack

Marine Spirit inflicts people of all ages both young and old with the Masturbation spirit for pleasure. It is unfortunate that believers' even pastors are in this evil act.

Masturbation causes stagnation in both male and female. It is a known fact that anyone in the act of masturbation does not succeed in whatever they lay their hands on especially in their business. Masturbation hinders blessings and no amount of prayers for financial breakthrough will manifest if you usually masturbate forpleasure.

Masturbation produces the spirit of lust and immorality.

Masturbation can weaken your sexual organ.

Masturbation brings your spiritual level very low Bad thoughts bring about Masturbation Foundational problemsproducemasturbation Watching porn films and magazines can make you masturbate

Evilassociationandplayingwithyourorgancan bring aboutmasturbation

Lack of sexual satisfaction can bring about masturbation

Masturbation separate you and God

Masturbation can steal your glory

Masturbation brings financial limitation and disgrace

Masturbation exposes a person to terrible attacks,

Masturbation leadstoweaknessoftheorgan

Masturbationdestroyslife completely.

Tostopmasturbationyoumustrepentandstay away fromsins

Prayer points against Masturbation

O Lord, help me to stop masturbation

OLord,helpmeovercomelustinJesusName.

I come against the demon of masturbation in my life in the name of Jesus Christ.

I rebuke all negative friends in the name of Jesus Christ.

I recover all my blessings stolen due to masturbation in Jesus Name.

I release myself from every marine bondage in the name of Jesus Christ.

Marine bondage, break and release me now, in Jesus name.

I burn to ashes by fire all arrow of masturbation hiding in my private part, in Jesus name.

O Lord, I destroy from my life all power of masturbation in Jesus Name.

I roast by fire all Serpent and scorpion of masturbation in my life in Jesus name.

I separate myself from every Spirit of masturbation programmed into my devices knowingly or unknowingly, In Jesus name.

Any satanic website calling my name to come and watch pornography, lose your grip over me and die, in Jesus name

O Lord, deliver me from Marine spirit in Jesus Name.

O Lord, all Properties of masturbation hiding around my life shall disappear forever, in Jesus name.

I render useless any negative power, supervising evil in my in Jesus name

Numberthreewaystodiscoveryouareunderthe control of a marine spirit is through Pornography.

Pornography is from Marine spirit and is a very bad spirit which leads to full demonic possession Pornography is fully practiced among the teenagers.pornography is very common among j the sexuallydeprivedtojustifytheirbehavior.

Pornography can create a distorted vision of intimacy making it nearly impossible to maintain a real romantic relationship.

Pornography is difficult to quit except by the divine intervention

Please note that anybody addicted to pornography will almost always masturbate as regularly as he watches porn so the correlation is direct.

How to avoid pornography

Acknowledge the fact that pornography is a problem. If truly you want to get out of pornography you need to acknowledge the problem before you can make any real effort towards overcoming it. You just have to admit you have a problem before profoundingsolution to it.

To get out of pornography you must avoid privacy and idleness. Anyone that is idle may be tempted to watch porn. Ones you avoid the above the urge to watch pornography will disappear gradually. So, avoid being alone today and most importantly rearrange all the computers and other devices you access porn through to the public area of the house especially in the sitting room, where everyone in the house will be able to view your activities.

Another way to get out of pornography is to engage yourself in meaningful activities such as exercising, gardening, playing with your children, etc. You could also engage in activities that take you out of the house or simply pay a visit to your friends and love ones each time you fill like engaging in the evil act.

Another way to get out of pornography is to acquire more knowledge or simply read your Bible every day. Read books that will improve your life or living standard will put away pornography in you. If you are serious about overcoming this addiction, you need to get your hands on as many resources as you can. You could also search online for educational resources that may help you better understand your problem and look into various techniques and methods that people have employed in the past.

Prayer points against pornography

O Lord, my Father forgive me all my sins and all the sins I committed relating to pornography, Father has mercy on me.

O Lord, cleanse my mind and my heart from images that have been imprinted there. I pray that you would renew my mind with images of you on the cross dying for my sins.

O Lord, the urge to serve and obey your word, please give it on to me.

I come against the demon of seduction, pornography, incubus, succubus and any other spirits that have attached themselves to me in Jesus Name.

O Lord, keep my mind free from evil and lustful thoughts in Jesus Name.

O Lord, Free me from a spirit of rejection and from pride.

O Lord, let Holy Spirit guide my steps, guard my heart, make my will Your will in Jesus Name.

Let us take a look at how marine Spirits Operate? Marine spirits possess and use monitoring powers to monitor and operate on their victims. Marine Spirits possess well-organized networks that can infiltrate anywhere.

Marine spirits use marine chains and padlocks to chain and padlock different areas of a person's life and destiny.

Marine spirits operate inside water and fire arrows of sickness, insanity, and poverty from there into people's lives.

Marine spirits transfer their materials into people by their agents through such avenues as sex, food, and sharing of clothes and other personal effects.

Marine spirits use the power of sex and other avenues to pollute people.

Marine spirits specialize in using images to manipulate and control peoples life.

Marine spirits are into a various category, they are marine priests, marine snakes, and other marine animals.

Marine spirits operate from marine altars which they use to manipulate, bewitch, and afflict their victims.

Marine spirits use their power to control and regulate nations anyhow they like.

Marine spirit manipulates families, and individuals in whatever way they want.
Marine spirits can inflict sickness into peoples body especially the ones that defy medical treatment.
Marine spirits are delicate and dangerous to the point that they have prisons and courts under the water where they imprison their victims and issue a judgment on them.
Marine spirits have their own burial ground where they bury their victims.
I reject any gift from marine agents in the name of Jesus Christ.
Marine agents are very fast in their operation and they steal precious things from people.
Marine spirits specialize in stealing breakthroughs, wealth, virtues, etc
Marine agents specialize in transferring sickness from their victims to another one.
They can also transfer bad luck, untimely death, sickness and other things from their own lives to the lives of others.
Marine spirit agents live a very long life by using the lives of others to elongate their own lives.
Marine agents pose as false prophets, ministers, and pastors to perpetuate their evil act.
Marine agents are most common in white garment churches.

Marine spirits can initiate people through eating their food, having sex with them, sharing clothes and personal property with them.

Marine spirits can be contacted through

Bathing with polluted waters at birth or with concoctions from the waters

Marine spirits can also be contacted through satanically inspired music and Evil association through carelessfriendship

When you reveal your secrets to marine agents throughtalkative, youcanbecontacted.

When you carelessly throw into the water things from your body.

Conducting night vigil by the river and burning incenseandcandlescancontactMarinespirits.

When you bury your placenta in the waters could attract Marine spirits.

Prayer points against marine spirits 1

Scripture: Revelation 17: 1 And there came one of the seven angels which had the seven vials, and talked with me, saying unto me, Come hither; I will shew unto thee the judgment of the great whore that sitteth upon many waters: 2 with whom the kings of the earth have committed fornication, and the inhabitants of the earth have been made drunk with the wine of her fornication.

Prayer points, Midnight Prayers

I reject every marine witchcraft militating against my life in Jesus Name.

I destroy every Marine deposit in my body by the power in the blood of Jesus Christ.

I separate myself from every stubborn marine spirit spouse, by the power in the blood of Jesus, i

I destroy every marine item in my possession, in the name of Jesus.

I reject any serpent dispatched against me from the waters in Jesus Name.

I reject any marine agent burning evil candles and incense against me, in Jesus Name.

I challenge my body with the fire of the Holy Ghost, and command every marine spirit, residing in my body to manifest and die, in Jesus' name.

I break by fire every evil covenant, binding me with water spirits, by the power in the blood of Jesus Christ.

I break every evil association between me and marine spirits, by the power in the blood of Jesus Christ.

I reject every evil dedication, made by my parents on any satanic altar in Jesus Name.

I reject every satanic guard assigned to my life from the marine kingdom in Jesus name.

I reject every satanic instrument from the marine kingdom, planted inside my bodyin Jesus Name.

I purge my body with every hidden serpent, in my body in Jesus Name.

I destroy by the power in the blood of Jesus Christ, every unconscious association with marine spirit, in Jesus name.

I cast every marine spirit out of my life, in the name of Jesus.

I uproot by fire every foundation of marine spirit in my life, in the name of Jesus Christ.

I reject every activity of the queen of the coast in my life, in Jesus Name.

O Lord, let confusion, chaos strike every river, water or sea, monitoring my life, by the power in the blood of Jesus Christ.

I break by the power in the blood of Jesus Christ, any evil soul tie covenant between me and water spirits.

I break by the power in the blood of Jesus Christ, every evil dedication of my life to water spirits.

I reject every satanic water spirits dominating and ruling over my life, in the name of Jesus.

I release my marriage by fire from every satanic water spirit holding my marriage in bondage in Jesus Name.

I decree and I declare that every stubborn marine spirit holding my progress and prosperity in bondage to lose your hold in Jesus Name.

By the power in the blood of Jesus Christ, I unseat every satanic marine spirit sitting upon my destiny in the name of Jesus Christ.

By the power in the blood of Jesus Christ, I break every binding marriage covenant between me and water spirits, in Jesus Name.

I break by fire, every evil zeal of the family idols over my life in the name of Jesus Christ.

I consume by fire any material in my body deposited on the altar of marine powers in the name of Jesus Christ.

I reject the water spirits drinking my prosperity, in the name of Jesus Christ.

I release my destiny from every satanic prison inside the waters in the name of Jesus Christ.

I release my breakthroughs from every satanic prison inside the waters in the name of Jesus Christ.

O Lord, I open now my womb locked up in the marinekingdominthenameofJesusChrist.

O Lord, I open now my marriage locked up in the marinekingdominthenameofJesusChrist.

O Lord, I open now by fire my prosperity locked up in the marine kingdom in the name of Jesus Christ.

O Lord, I open now by fire my job locked up in the marinekingdominthenameofJesusChrist. OLord,I opennowbyfiremystarslockedupin themarine kingdominthenameofJesusChrist O Lord, I destroy by fire, the cage of stagnancy in the marine kingdom holding my life and my destiny in Jesus Name

By the power in the blood of Jesus Christ, every spirit of infirmity eating my flesh and drinking my blood shalldiebyfireinthenameofJesus Christ.

I open now by fire every road of progress and prosperity that marine spirits have locked up againstme in the name of Jesus Christ.

Thank God for answered prayers.

Prayers against Marine Spirits 2

Scripture: Genesis 1:6-7 And God said, "Let there be a vault between the waters to separate water from water." 7 So God made the vault and separated the water under the vault from the water above it. And it was so.

Prayer points, Night prayers before bedtime

In this night prayers, I cover myself and my family with the blood of Jesus Christ.

This night, I shall restore the lost glory of my family line in the name of Jesus Christ.

I bind and paralyze the activities of marine spirits in my life in the name of Jesus Christ.

Every strongman in charge of my womb shall di in the name of Jesus Christ.

By the power in the blood of Jesus Christ, I close firmly all the doorways of the enemy into my life be closed in Jesus Name.

Tonight, I shall vomit all poison planted into my womb by marine agents in Jesus Name.

I reject the poison that enters my body while eating in the dream in Jesus Name.

I reject the poison that enters my body while drinking dirty water in the dream in Jesus Name. I come against all evil plantations in my business to come out with all their roots in the name of Jesus.

I break by fire all problems in my life created by marine spirits in the name of Jesus.

I soak my body, in the blood of Jesus

Tonight any evil arrow fiery red into my life should go back to the sender in the name of Jesus Christ.

O Lord, tonight Let the thunder of God strike any marine spirit planning to attack me in the dream in Jesus Name.

O Lord, move me to the next level in Jesus Name.

O Lord, anointing to excel in life fall upon me now in the name of Jesus Christ.

Dealing and defeating the Marine Kingdom as a whole

It is a known fact that when dealing with Marine Spirit you have to be prepared and applied the Knowledge you acquired to ensure maximum victory. You don't engage in warfare with Marine Spirit without adequate and application of knowledge.

Among the three demonic kingdoms, Marine kingdom believes that they are the strongest among them. The head of the marine kingdom is the queen of the coast with their headquarters in India. The marine kingdom is responsible for the following

1. Chronic angerpeople
2. Deadineverythinginaman's life, eg, dead brain, dead organs, dead spiritual life.
3. The weakening of pastors power to perform a miracle or cast out demons
4. Inability to get married on time
5. Frequent divorce
6. Bankruptcy
7. Spirit wife
8. Spirit husband
9. Sex in the dream

Prophetic Declarations

The only person who can set the standards of your life is you. Marine Spirit cannot stop you in achieving your goals in life, it all depends on you. Don't let anyone else define your standards. The world is round but some say it's cruel, no matter what kind of life you have. Keep your dignity intact. I pray this day, God shall take away your pain and despair of yesterday and any unpleasant memories shall be replaced with your glorious promise of new hope in Jesus name. Amen

. I pray for you today and ask God to make you greater than you are, show you more ways than you know and make your future brighter than you can ever think of. May the beauty of God's love touch your heart and may all that you wish for come to pass in Jesus mighty name.

The Lord that destroyed the garment of shame assigned to blind Bartimaeus shall make shame a stranger to your life in the name of Jesus. You shall not miss your divine allocation of blessing, breakthrough, healing, glory, and favor in Jesus name. May the labors of your enemy receive double failure in the mighty name of Jesus Christ.

Prayer points to defeat Water Spirit My body hears the word of the Lord, reject water spirit in Jesus name.

Today I put an end of all water spirit operation in my life in Jesus Name.

I reject totally Laziness and procrastination in my life in Jesus Name.

O Lord, fill me with your power to defeat water spirit in my life in Jesus Name

O, Lord. Angel of death will not visit my house in Jesus Name.

O Lord, my enemy will not defeat me in Jesus Name.

O Lord, the Sun of my life shall not listen to the voice of water spirit in Jesus Name

O Lord, I shall locate the right people at the right time in Jesus Name.

O Lord, arise and judge every stubborn marine agent in Jesus Name.

O Lord, every deceit in my life shall die in Jesus Name.

I reject totally, delay in my life in Jesus Name.

I reject disbelief, dishonesty, discouragement and distractions in Jesus Name.

Defeating Marine Spirit by becoming the Oracle of God

Scriptures: Psalm 5:8: Lead me, O LORD, in thy righteousness because of mine enemies; make thy way straight before my face.

Scriptures: Psalm 25:14: The secret of the LORD is with them that fear him, and he will shew them his covenant.

PrayerpointstoovercomeMarine powers

I bind and cast out every marine power slowing down my progress in Jesus Name.

I destroy every spirit of fear in my life in Jesus Name.

By the power in the blood of Jesus Christ, I command every marine power to lose their whole in Jesus Name.

By the power in the blood of Jesus Christ, I

.I reject every marine agent projection of my life in JesusName.

My breakthrough shall not pass me by in Jesus Name.

O Lord, I receive the oracle of God to enable me to defeat marine spirit in Jesus name.

By the power in the blood of Jesus Christ, I receive power to arrest every marine power planning to arrest me in Jesus Name.

O Lord, come upon my life Power of spiritual responsibility and self-denial, in Jesus Name.

I invite into my life to the Spirit of revelation and wisdom to defeat the marine kingdom in Jesus Name.

O Lord, deliver me from the bondage marine spirit in Jesus Name.

O Lord, reveal openly every operation of marine spirit concerning my life in Jesus Name.

O Lord, expose every marine spirit operation in my household in Jesus name.

Prophetic Declarations

If you have been dealt with or defeated by Marine Agents, you have not failed totally. I want you to know that there is still hope for you. Failure is not an event, it's an opinion. The fact that you failed in one thing doesn't mean that your life is over. There is no failure or defeat with God; therefore, you can't fail in life. This is how every child of God must see life. I pray this day, Godly freedom will become your possession and any marine agent agenda against you and your family is dispersed into the trash and you loosed from bondage into freedom to fulfill God- given assignments in Jesus powerful name. Amen.

Today, the LORD God will manifest His glorious power in your situation and make you a Point of Reference, a Channel of Blessings, a Symbol of

Success, a Vessel of Testimonies and a Pillar of Joy. God will speak for you. Heaven will open for your sake and every blessing from above will locate you. Whatever you say or do shall be seasoned with favor. His presence shall be your abode in Jesus mighty name. Amen

7 Days Fasting and Prayer Programs to Destroy the Activities of Water Spirits: Day one

Prayer points to destroy the activities of Water Spirits

I bind every demon coming out of the marine kingdom in Jesus Name.

I wash clean every dirtiness blocking my communication pipe with the living God by the power in the blood of Jesus Christ.

I receive power to operate with sharp spiritual eyes that cannot be deceived by the marine spirit in the name of Jesus Christ.

Let the glory and the power of the Almighty God, fall upon my life in a mighty way, in the name of Jesus.

O Lord, I remove my name from the book of the Marine Kingdom in the name of Jesus Christ.

I am filled with the well of salvation and anointing, in the name of Jesus Christ.

O Lord, I refuse to fall under the manipulation of the marine spirit, in the name of Jesus Christ.

I stand against all the activities of Marine spirit seeking to manipulate my decision in Jesus Name.

I bind the activities of Lust in Jesus Name.

I bind the activities of water spirit manipulation in the dream in Jesus Name.

I bind the activities of demonic manipulations in the dream in Jesus Name.

I bind ungodly infatuation in my life in Jesus Name.

I bind Spiritual blindness and deafness in my life in Jesus Name.

Holy Spirit, open my eyes and help me to make the right decision, in the name of Jesus.

Holy Ghost fire, take over my soul, spirit and body

By the power in the blood of Jesus Christ, I set on fire every water spirit object in my body, in Jesus Name.

I flush out every water spirit object moving in my body, in Jesus name.

By the power in the blood of Jesus Christ, break and scatter every covenant tying me to water spirit in Jesus Name.

I break and release myself from every water spirit dedication and covenant in Jesus Name.

I break and scatter to pieces anything connecting me to water spirit, in Jesus Name.

I burn to ashes anything water spirit has planted into my body, in Jesus Name.

I set on fire and burn to ashes every property of the water spirit in my possession, in Jesus Name. I burn to ashes all Marine spirit property in my possession in Jesus Name.

By the power in the blood of Jesus Christ, I cut off any Water spirit agent following me about, in Jesus Name.

I vomit by fire anything water spirit agent has given me to eat, in Jesus Name.

Prophetic Declarations

No matter the activities of water spirit in your life, only you can make yourself happy. I think happiness comes when you finally realize that it comes from inside "you". No one else can make you truly happy unless you are happy with yourself and your own life. Not a relationship, not a career, not "things". The moment you say "I am happy" to yourself, is the moment you knew you are......... I pray this day, may God's blessings flow through you and touch the lives of everyone you meet.

Proverbs 13:12 says, Hope deferred makes the heart sick, but when the desire is fulfilled, it is a tree of life. I decree today, every marine power that is prolonging your Hope and your Breakthrough from being fulfilled shall scatter unto desolation in Jesus Name. The power of the Most High God shall disgrace every opposition to your Heavenly Crown, and He will destroy every water spirit that is bent in wasting your destiny in Jesus Name. You shall live to glorify God.

Day Two: Resisting the Water Spirit

What does it mean to resist the water spirit? It means to strive against the water spirit
It means to act against the water spirit It means to oppose the water spirit
It means to stand against the water spirit It means to abstain from the water spirit It means to assault the water spirit
It means to battle the water spirit
It means to confront the water spirit It means to combat the water spirit
It means to turn down the water spirit It means to hinder the water spirit
It means to defy the water spirit
It means to fight back the water spirit It means to keep from the water spirit

Therefore, if you don't want water spirit to take control of your life, you have to resist it. If you don't know how to resist, you would not be able to fight back.

Please pray all the prayer points below as they will go a long way in helping you to resist the water spirit.

Prayer points

I resist and reject and scatter every assignment given to me by the water spirit in Jesus name.

I resist, reject and burn to ashes by the power in the blood of Jesus Christ anything representing

queen of the coast and queen of heaven in my body
I resist and set on fire every water spirit curses hindering my destiny, in Jesus Name.
I resist, set on fire and burn to ashes the water spirit altar manipulating my life, in Jesus name.
I resist, set on fire and burn to ashes every water spirit altar in Jesus Name.
I resist, break into pieces and scatter every marriage between me and water spirit, in Jesus Name.
I resist and break every bondage, water spirit has put me into in Jesus Name.
I resist and break every curse water spirit has placed on me and my entire family in Jesus Name.
I resist and cut off the water spirit claiming me as my wife/husband, in Jesus Name.
I break and cut off myself from every water spirit dedication and covenant in Jesus Name.
I resist and break every link between me and the water spirit in Jesus Name.
By the power in the blood of Jesus Christ, I resist and cancel every decision water spirit has made against me and my entire family in Jesus Name
I scatter into pieces every work of the marine kingdom targeted against me and my entire family in the name of Jesus Christ.

I resist and burn to ashes sacrifices raised against me and my family by Marine agent in Jesus Name.

I resist and burn to ashes all the things the water kingdom is using to fight me, by the power in the blood of Jesus Christ.

I resist, burn to ashes water spirit monitoring garget used to monitor me and my entire family in Jesus Name

I resist, burn to ashes anything representing me in the marine kingdom in Jesus Name.

I claim back all my lost, stolen and delayed blessings by water spirits in Jesus Name.

By the power in the blood of Jesus Christ, I destroy every water spirit food in my blood in Jesus Name.

Any marine planning to destroy my destiny die now, in Jesus name.

By the power in the blood of Jesus Christ, I command any marine power stealing my virtues secretly, to die in Jesus Name.

By the power in the blood of Jesus Christ. I break every covenant I have entered into with the marine spirit in Jesus Name.

Prophetic Declarations

When you worship God Almighty, He will definitely guide and protect you from the activities of water spirits. They cannot defeat you. The able hands of God Almighty will Guide,

Protect and Pilot you in the right direction. He will keep you, bless you and make His face to shine upon you. He will keep you out of any disaster and all things shall work for your good. Rise up like a Lion and dominate your environment by the special grace of God Almighty.

Tonight take advantage of the authority you have in God's word. At your decree, mountains will move and water spirit will flee. This means you don't have an excuse to continue playing the victim. The only person standing in your way is you. Get up and speak the word. You are victorious in Jesus name.

Everything happens for a reason. Sometimes, the bad things that happen to us will lead us down the road to some of the best things we could have ever dreamed of. Never lose hope because miracles happen every day. I pray this day, Almighty God in his infinite mercy will perfect all that concerns you and take off every policy stopping you from moving forward in Jesus name. Amen.

Day Three: I recover my Breakthroughs and Blessings from the water spirit

Prayer points

Water spirit crying against my breakthroughs break by the power of the blood of Jesus Christ. O Lord, I claim all by lost breakthroughs and blessings in Jesus Name.

I reject any marine spirit planning my demotion in Jesus Name.

I reject any marine power working against my blessings and breakthroughs, such power shall die in Jesus Name.

O Lord, I recover my lost glory from the hands of marine spirit in Jesus Name.

By tt he power in the blood of Jesus Christ, I recover all blessings and breakthroughs I lost through my mother's carelessness in Jesus Name.

O Lord, restore back to me the breakthroughs and blessings I lost by being carried by any marine spirit agent hand in Jesus Name.

O Lord, deliver me from marine agent midwife which gave me my first birth and stole my blessings and breakthroughs, in Jesus name.

O Lord, deliver my breakthroughs and blessings from the marine agents I have slept with in the name of Jesus.

O Lord, deliver my breakthroughs and blessings from all the marine kingdom in Jesus Name.

O Lord, I am free from every marine spirit pronouncement against my life and destiny

By the power in the blood of Jesus Christ, I paralyze every force of affliction against my body in Jesus Name.

All marine agents come out of your hiding places in the name of Jesus

I paralyze every marine king installed against me by the power in the blood of Jesus Christ.

O Lord, anoint me with your power in Jesus Name.

O Lord, let your healing power circulate into my body in the name of Jesus

O Lord, I deliver my head from every pollution in Jesus Name.

Lord, make the impossible possible for me in the name of Jesus.

O Lord, make a way for me where there is no way in Jesus Name.

I reject every assignment and weapon of the water spirit against me in the name of Jesus Christ.

O, Lord. I reverse every destiny destroyed by polygamy in Jesus name.

I command every water spirit working against my destiny, to die, in the name of Jesus Christ.

I reject every marine power assigned against my destiny, in Jesus Name

I reject every marine power trying to re-program my life, in the name of Jesus Christ.

I reject every rearrangement of my destiny by a marine spirit in the name of Jesus Christ.

I reject every activity of marine power against my spiritual life in Jesus Name

By the power in the blood of Jesus Christ, I release all my imprisoned benefits in Jesus Name.

Prophetic Declarations

The palm tree is a unique tree because of its importance and usefulness. While other trees are treated with levity, the palm tree is not. That is why I decree into your life that where others are underpriced, undervalued or underestimated, you will be rated highly and valued extremely. Everything that comes out from you, just like a palm tree, will be highly in demand. You will not lose your value, credibility, integrity, and importance in the mighty name of Jesus.

As you call on God Almighty today, HIS lovingkindness shall not depart from you. Every mountain confronting you shall melt before the fire of the Lord. God shall empower you and you shall be far from any form of evil. Henceforth, whoever assembles against your destiny or against your family shall fall for your sake Disparagers will always act blind to what God is doing in your life because they live in delusion. Don't take offense, and never become one yourself. Be confident of one thing, He that has begun a good work in you is faithful to complete it. Keep it in your consciousness, God is at work in your life, that's what matters!

On this beautiful day, I urge you to stop comparing yourself to other people. We are all uniquely different and our journeys are not the same. Define your own success, chase your own dreams and be the best that you can be.

I pray this day, every enemy that is trembling your life and disturbing your prosperity, they shall be powerless before you today in the powerful name of Jesus. Amen.

DAY FOUR: DELIVERANCE FROM WATER SPIRIT BONDAGE

Prayer points

I release myself from every water spirit bondage in the name of Jesus Christ.

I release myself from any inherited water spirit bondage in the name of Jesus Christ.

By the power in the blood of Jesus Christ, flush out from my system every inherited satanic deposit.

I reject every inherited water spirit covenants in the name of Jesus Christ.

I break and lose myself from every inherited water spirit curse in the name of Jesus Christ.

I paralyze all water spirits attached to my life in Jesus Name.

I break and lose myself from every form of marine power bewitchment in the name of Jesus Christ.

By the power in the blood of Jesus Christ, I uproot the evil foundational plantation

I release myself from every marine spirit and control in the name of Jesus Christ.

O Lord, restore me back to the original design you made for my life.

I curse every curse issued me by a marine agent in Jesus Name.

By the power in the blood of Jesus Christ, I destroy the evil authority over my life and business in the name of Jesus Christ.

I break the backbones and destroy the roots of every water spirit that is working against my life and destiny in Jesus Name.

I roast every seat of marine spirit in my household in the name of Jesus Christ.

O Lord, Let the thunder of God strike and scatter beyond redemption, the foundation of water spirit in my household in the name of Jesus Christ.

I expose by fire, every hiding place and secret place of the marine agent in my family, in the name of Jesus Christ.

Let every local and international witchcraft network of my household witches be shattered to pieces in Jesus name.

Every marine power harboring enchantment against me, vomit them, by the power in the blood of Jesus Christ.

I destroy by fire every marine spirit pot of darkness seated against my life, in the name of Jesus Christ.
I reject every marine power cooking my progress in an evil pot in Jesus Name.
I withdraw by fire every marine spirit money spent on my behalf, in Jesus Name.
Every marine spirit law over my life, vanish by fire, in the name of Jesus.
Every marine spirit verdicts against my life, turn againstyoursender,inthenameofJesusChrist. I break every curse of bitterness issued against my life by water spirit in the name of Jesus Christ.
I frustrate the communication system of my household marine spirit in Jesus name.
I dismantle by fire very marine spirit network working against my prosperity in Jesus Name.
I break every altar of marine spirit and familiar spirit, in the name of Jesus Christ.
I break into pieces every evil mirrors used to monitor my life break to pieces, in the name of Jesus
Prophetic Declarations
Jesus went through challenges, so also are the great men and women of God in the Bible, and they are not defeated. This morning, I pray for you and your family, whatever challenges you are going through, I pray that you shall not be

defeated by the devil in Jesus name. Every evil bullet targeted against you, your family, your destiny, your business or career shall be returned to sender in Jesus name.

For your sake, the Lord will arise and scatter all the enemies of your breakthrough, He will open the windows of heaven and pour out spiritual, emotional. physical and financial blessings onto you today and always in Jesus name. Amen.

Associate with people who are happy. Seek the companionship of those who can give you new points of view, renewed hope, and more meaningful life.

Thank you, Lord for the grace to witness the light of a new day in the land of the living.........

I pray for you this morning in accordance with Psalm 20 vs 4; the Almighty God will satisfy you with the desires of your heart and fulfill all your counsel. Anointing for uncommon favor, success, breakthrough, blessings, happiness, shall fall upon you today. Your life will be a reference point of success to others and God will keep a permanent smile on your face. All your endeavors today will yield bountiful harvests and your heart will be filled with unlimited Joy in Jesus mighty name

Attract others with your character and not with your appearance. Those who love you for your character will always remain with you. I pray this day, your ears shall hear good news and you shall not hear the voice of the enemy in Jesus name. Amen.

Many of us have knocked on many doors while some of us are afraid to begin knocking. Afraid of more insults or afraid that you may get too many negative responses. The fear to try again remains heavy. Whether for a certain job, starting your own business or approaching someone. Be bold and very courageous. The enemy will use fear as a strong hold over you to keep you stagnated. I bless you today with the Favor of the Almighty God. That today you will not be afraid to knock. Favor will be connected to that knock. Today your time has come to knock. Knock that will put you forward. Jesus wasn't afraid to go down Judah again even thou the Jews sought to stone him. It's time to go down there again. Even though you may not feel to. Don't follow your feelings it will only point you to fear.

DayFive:RecoveringofmyStolen Blessings

Prayer points to recover my stolen blessings

Anything in me supporting marine spirit embargo on my finances, disappear in Jesus Name.

I recover all my stolen blessings from marine agent in Jesus Name.

I cancel every agreement made by my ancestors with marine powers, in the name of Jesus Christ. You wicked marine powers in my father's house, die, in the name of Jesus Christ.

I destroy every agreement I have with water spirit in my family in Jesus Name.

I reject every evil word spoken by marine spirits to my destiny in Jesus Name.

O Lord, take away the strength of my enemies especially marine powers in Jesus Name.

O Lord, by the power in the blood of Jesus Christ, my enemies especially marine powers shall be disgraced.

O Lord, I shall overtake all my enemies in every area of my life in Jesus Name.

Any marine power holding the key of my elevation shall receive double failure in Jesus Name.

O Lord, give me the power to fulfill my divine agenda in Jesus Name.

I decree and I declare that any marine power that would work to re-build my Jericho, shall die, in the name of Jesus Christ.

O Lord, I refuse to live under any marine spirit control, in the name of Jesus Christ.

I scatter by every satanic check-point mounted against my destiny this year, in the name of Jesus Christ.

Lord, let great deliverance begin to take place in my life now, in the name of Jesus

I take back everything the marine agent has stolen from my life in the name of Jesus Christ.

I command every devourer and wasters of fortune, including marine spirit to depart from my life in the name of Jesus Christ.

Prophetic Declarations

In three of the Gospels, we learn about a guy with leprosy who comes to Jesus and says, "If You are willing, You can heal me and make me clean" (Matthew 8:1-4; Mark 1:40-45, Luke 5:12- 16). In response, Jesus does something interesting, and it's recorded in each account: He touches the man. While touching a person with leprosy may seem like a nice humanitarian gesture to us, it was probably scandalous for Jesus.

As a matter of law, Jesus made Himself unclean when He touched someone with leprosy. But that didn't stop Him. He didn't have anything to worry about.

Jesus wasn't in danger of being infected by the man's brokenness. Jesus was the contagious one. His goodness and righteousness infected anyone who opened up to Him. And with just one touch, the man's leprosy was gone.

As you wake up today, your movement will be full of grace, favor, and accomplishments. May the day bring to you good news. The oil of grace upon your life will never run dry. The Lord will make everything work well for you. Just like the Eagle, you will fly. Like Gold, you will be valued. Like the Sun, you shall shine bright. Like the river, you shall flow unlimitedly. Like the Palm Tree, you shall flourish and Like Money, you shall be useful. Today and beyond, peace and prosperity shall be your portion and your joy shall multiply greatly in Jesus Mighty name.

You probably don't have leprosy, but there are plenty of other things that make us feel unclean. Maybe, for you, it's an addictive behavior, an unforgettable experience with childhood abuse, a failure at work, or a relationship that's damaged because of mistakes you made. You might not want to reveal it, talk about it, or otherwise deal with it; but hiding it only masks the symptoms.

Jesus wants to touch that every part of you. He's not afraid of it; and besides, He already knows about it anyway, so He's not going to think any less of you for it.

After you show Him your brokenness, you can pray this simple prayer: "If You are willing, You can heal me and make me clean." He is willing, and in the end, the most broken parts of your life will be what reveals His glory in you most beautifully. Let me conclude with this favorite scripture of mine - "Let us, therefore, come boldly to the throne of grace, that we may obtain mercy and find grace to help in time of need" (Hebrews4:16).

Day Six

Prayer Points: Victory over Marine Spirits

I break every curse of bitterness issued against my life by marine spirits, in the name of Jesus Christ.

By the power in the blood of Jesus Christ, every internal and external marine power working against my life, strike against yourselves to destruction, in Jesus name.

I command every vessel of marine spirit attack, to sleep the sleep of death, in the name of Jesus Christ.

O Lord put to shame every marine spirit that is against my business in Jesus Name

O Lord, let all satanic instruments used against mebe completelydestroyed,inJesusname.

I paralyze completely all marine spirit transactions against me in the name of Jesus Christ.

O Lord, I desire breakthroughs concerning victory over marine powers in the name of Jesus Christ

Lord, I desire breakthroughs concerning the total defeatofmarinepowersinJesusName

I remove my businesscareer from the dominion of the marine powers in Jesus Name.

1. I take authority over and over the binding of the strongman of financial failure.

Let every financial failure in my life receive termination now, in the name of Jesus.

Let every anti-progress altar fashioned against me be destroyed with the thunder fire of God, in Jesus name.

Let every marine power chasing away my blessings be paralyzed, in the name of Jesus Christ.

O Lord, Let every good thing eaten up by marine spirit be vomited now, in the name of Jesus Christ.

O Lord, give me the power to overcome all obstacles to my breakthroughs in the name of Jesus Christ.

O Lord, all my imprisoned and buried potentials by marine spirits begin to come forth now, in the name of Jesus Christ

Any program of marine powers in my house, I dismantle you by fire in the name of Jesus Christ. I stand against the powers of the wasters in the name of Jesus Christ.

Prophetic Declarations

Whatever you do today, make sure you keep your joy because it shall be your strength.

You are too close to your breakthrough to be sad.

I pray this day that all our heart desires be granted unto us. New levels, new directions that will lead us to things that will bring glory and not shame to hisname.RememberGodisclosetous when we draw ourselves close to him.
If the red sea can saw the glory of God and fled and river Jordan saw him and turned back, while mountain and hills skipped like lamb. it means your problem is nothinginGodsight,sodon'tbe weary orfret.
Henceforth your red sea, mountains, and hills that confronted you in the past and the one planning to confront you shall bow to the glory of the Lord. Your problem is not so hard as they appear as long as you secure God presence, His divine ability is secure for you, you may not believe this, God has approved your heart request
Today, stick with this with faith, you are the next that people will rejoice within Jesus name. Amen.
This morning, God Almighty will show you a secret that will rewrite your story. Wherever your name is mentioned it will be with honor and dignity.
I pray that God will always lead you and satisfy your needs in drylands. He will give strength to your bones, you will be like a garden that has plenty of water, like a spring that never goes dry and Victory shall be yours. I pray that

God will send you abundant grace to push you up to the ladder of sufficiency & no one will have the privilege to tell you sorry in life. Congratulation is your portion while testimony is your escort this week in Jesus mighty name.

Day Seven

Prayer points: Power against the marine Kingdom 1

I release myself from the activities of the marine kingdom in Jesus Name.

I paralyze every activity of the marine kingdom in the name of Jesus Christ.

All spirits in the marine kingdom rooted in spirit husband, come out of my life with all your roots in Jesusname.

I reject every anti-testimony, in the name of Jesus Christ.

By the power In the name of Jesus Christ, I shall be victorious over all the forces of darkness includingmarinespirit,inJesus'name.

I scatter completely every marine spirit gathered against my breakthrough, in the name of Jesus Christ.

By the power in the blood of Jesus Christ, I reject the spirit of the tail and I claim the spirit of the head, in the name of Jesus Christ.

I bind every marine spirit delegated to hinder the manifestations of my miracles, in the name of Jesus Christ.

Prophetic Declarations

Thank God it's another day. Glory be to God for his mercy and love for giving you another opportunity to be alive. I pray today that, the Almighty God will create a shield of protection around you and your family. May the provision, protection, and presence of God never depart from you and your household. I command every curse and covenant of impossibility over your life to break in the name of Jesus. Till date, how water gets inside the coconut remains a mystery. The source of your joy, , and happiness will remain a mystery to your enemies today and forever in Jesus Wonderful name. Amen

As you open up to Him, He will open you up to a new chapter of Holiness, Grace, Mercy, and Fulfillment. Good morning and have a blessed week.

Take a bold step in your life and make the necessary changes you have to make. Determine to go to a higher level. Don't allow small- mindedness to hinder you from being great. You can be all that God wants you to be if you focus on His ability and not your inability.

When God is about to deliver you, change your season or bring you into your Promised Land, He

also usually closes all other doors, hardens the hearts of people who can help you in the natural and leaves you in a place where when your manifestation happens, nobody can ever claim credit for it and you too will know that this is the Lord's doing and it is marvelous in your eyes. So the rejection and cutting off is a sign that you are about to step into your best days. Go ahead. Grit your teeth and step into it.
I pray this day that the most high God shall carry you on the eagle's wings above all barriers and He shall make every crooked path straight for you today and forever in Jesus mighty name. Amen.

As long as Jehovah God lives and reign forever; This month of May, God will have mercy upon you and His glory shall show forth in your life.
God will bless you with that divine key that opens heavens abundant resources. There shall be a continuous flow of money/riches into your coffer. You shall never be limited by the world economic crisis, neither shall you lack the wisdom to manage success. Because you have God, the best of all things of life shall be made available to you on earth.
This month, you shall enjoy maximum access to the heavenly and hidden treasures useful for your destiny and your glory. Every satanic

challenge against your health, marital joy, career/business and destiny shall be terminated and utterly destroyed. Everything that is sick in your life shall receive healing of the most High God in Jesus name. Amen.

Powerful Midnight prayers to totally destroy Marine spirits

Scriptures: Matthew 13:25: "While men slept, his enemy came and sowed tares among the wheat, and went his way."

Prayer points

In most cases, prayers are better prayed in the midnight in spiritual warfare or stubborn. The purpose of midnight prayers is to fight your battles and give you total victory over your enemies. If you want to destroy the activities of marine spirits, it is better down in the middle of the night.

Prayer points

O Lord, pass judgment by fire on all the spirits in the marine kingdom

I destroy every garment of marine spirit on my body, in Jesus Name.

By the power in the blood of Jesus Christ, I destroy every opportunity wasters, in Jesus Name.

By the power in the blood of Jesus Christ, I break any chain binding my finances, in Jesus Name.

Marine spirit-sponsored infirmities, die in Jesus Name.

I scatter every power of the night programmed against my progress, in Jesus Name.

I cut off every satanic malpractice over my family, in Jesus Name.

I burn to ashes every marine power assigned to use my life as a dumping ground, in Jesus Name. Every tongue anointed by the marine spirit to speak against my life, you are not my God, scatter in Jesus Nam

I break every yoke upon my hands, in Jesus name.

I break any curse issued against my hands, in Jesus Name.

I break-loose from my life, any power that has tied down my destiny, in Jesus Name.

Every marine power toying with my destiny shall die in Jesus Name.

I curse the spirit of backwardness, in Jesus Name.

Every marine kingdom register bearing my destiny, catch fire in Jesus Name.

Every marine power delaying the manifestation of my breakthroughs shall die in Jesus Name.

Every proclamation of the powers of the marine kingdom against my life shall die in Jesus Name.

I destroy every calendar of the enemy, working against my life, in Jesus Name.

O Lord, kill any evil command of the marine kingdom I have obeyed, in the name of Jesus.

O Lord, do not be tired of hearing me when I call upon you. O Lord, defeat marine spirit on my behalf
By the power in the blood of Jesus Christ, I break every witchcraft bondage in my life, in Jesus Name.
I arrest every astral projection against my life in the name of Jesus Christ.
Every witchcraft power that has set eyes on me, receive blindness in the name of Jesus Christ.
Every evil arrow in the marine kingdom assigned against my life shall backfire in the name of Jesus Christ.
Every marine power stealing my promotion shall die in the name of Jesus Christ.
Every Camera of darkness, taking my pictures in the dark world, shall catch fire in the name of Jesus Christ.
Every inherited marine power assigned to waste my destiny, come out now In the name of Jesus. Every arrow of marine powers fired into my prosperity, shall die in the name of Jesus Christ. Every marine power drawing my virtues die in the name of Jesus Christ
Every marine Power assigned to make my life useless shall die in the name of Jesus Christ.
Any marine power disconnecting me from the virtues of the Lord shall die in the name of Jesus.

Any marine Power assigned to push me to the back shall expire in the name of Jesus Christ.
Every marine power assigned to disorganize my life shall die in the name of Jesus.

Roundup prayers against marine witchraft andwaterspirits

Scriptures: PSALM 8:4-8, Isa.27

Prayer points

In faith, I come against evil strongholds of any marine kingdom.

Any marine power under any water against my life, receive immediate judgment of fire, in the name of Jesus Christ.

O Lord, Let every evil altar underwater be destroyed in the name of Jesus Christ.

O Lord, every priest ministering at an evil altar against me inside any water, shall die, in the name of Jesus Christ.

Any marine power under any river or sea remotely-controlling my life, be destroyed by the power in the name of Jesus Christ.

O Lord, let every marine spirit that has introduced spirit husband/wife or child in my dreams be roasted by fire, in the name of Jesus Christ.

Every marine spirit agent attached to my marriage to frustrate it shall die in the name of Jesus Christ.

Every marine spirit agent assigned to attack my friancés through the dream die in the name of Jesus Christ.

O Lord, Let the thunderbolts of God locate and destroy every marine witchcraft covens in the name of Jesus Christ.

1. Any water spirits from my village or place of my birth, practicing witchcraft against me shall die in the name of Jesus Christ.

Any marine power holding any of my blessings in bondage, release them now in the name of Jesus Christ.

O Lord I lose my mind and soul from the bondage of marine witches in the name of Jesus Christ.

O Lord, I command every arrow shot into my life from under any water by marine spirit, to go back to their sender in the name of Jesus Christ. I roast by fire, any evil material transferred into my body through contact with any marine spirit agent in the name of Jesus

I reject any evil name given to me under any water, by the power in the name of Jesus Christ

I roast by fire every image constructed under any water to manipulate me, in the name of Jesus Christ.

I reverse by the power in the blood of Jesus Christ any evil is ever done against me through marine power oppression in the name of Jesus Christ.

O Lord, I disgrace by fire every marine spirit present in my family, in the name of Jesus Christ. Every strongman from the marine kingdom holding me captive shall die in the name of Jesus Christ.

I flush out every deposit of marine spirit in my life by the power in the blood of Jesus Christ.

I command every marine power blocking my moving forward to die in the name of Jesus Christ.

I release my life from the grip of marine spirit, in the name of Jesus Christ

Contact Us

For further spiritual help please email info@olusolacoker.com

For Christian news, free ebooks, articles, prayers etc please visitwww.olusolacoker.com

www.ingramcontent.com/pod-product-compliance
Ingram Content Group UK Ltd.
Pitfield, Milton Keynes, MK11 3LW, UK
UKHW021925190726
13853UKWH00002B/843